Rebecca Faulkner | **How to get ahead in**

Leisure & Tourism

www.raintreepublishers.co.uk

Visit our website to find out more information about **Raintree** books.

To order:

☎ Phone 44 (0) 1865 888113

🖹 Send a fax to 44 (0) 1865 314091

🖵 Visit the Raintree bookshop at **www.raintreepublishers.co.uk**
to browse our catalogue and order online.

First published in Great Britain by Raintree,
Halley Court, Jordan Hill, Oxford OX2 8EJ,
part of Harcourt Education.
Raintree is a registered trademark of
Harcourt Education Ltd.

Editorial: Melanie Waldron, Lucy Beevor,
and Kate Buckingham
Design: David Poole and Calcium
Illustrations: Geoff Ward
Picture Research: Melissa Allison
and Fiona Orbell
Production: Huseyin Sami

Originated by Chroma Graphics
Printed and bound in China
by South China Printing Company

10 digit ISBN 1 406 20447 1 (hardback)
13 digit ISBN 978 1 406 20447 6
11 10 09 08 07
10 9 8 7 6 5 4 3 2 1

10 digit ISBN 1 406 20459 5 (paperback)
13 digit ISBN 978 1 406 20459 9
12 11 10 09 08
10 9 8 7 6 5 4 3 2 1

British Library Cataloguing in Publication Data
Faulkner, Rebecca
Leisure and Tourism. – (How to get ahead in)
338.4'791'02341
A full catalogue record for this book is
available from the British Library.

Acknowledgements
The publishers would like to thank the
following for permission to reproduce
photographs: Alamy pp. 26 (ACE STOCK
LIMITED), 5 (Arch White), 10 (Art Kowalsky), 33,
47 (BananaStock), 19 (Chris A. Crumley), 9
(David White), 15 (ICP), 27 (Mike Greenslade), 40
(Photofusion Picture Library); Corbis pp. 44
(Franco Vogt), 51 (LWA-Stephen Welstead), 21
(Matthias Kulka), 12 (Natalie Fobes), 8 (Royalty-
Free), 7 (zefa/Pete Saloutos); Corbis pp. 51 (LWA-
Stephen Welstead); Education Photos pp. 23, 46
(John Walmsley); Getty Images pp. 35, 36
(Photodisc), 4, 20, 29, 32 (Stone), 50 (Taxi);
Harcourt Education Ltd p. 30 (Tudor
Photography); Photographer's Choice p. 24 (Getty
Images); reportdigital.co.uk pp. 17 (David
Bocking), 37 (David Mansell); Ski Club of Great
Britain p. 14.

Cover photograph of flippers reproduced with
permission of Getty Images/Imagebank/
John Kelly.

The publishers would like to thank Sue Finch
MSc (Tourism) for her assistance in the
preparation of this book.

Every effort has been made to contact
copyright holders of any material reproduced
in this book. Any omissions will be rectified in
subsequent printings if notice is given to the
publishers.

Contents

Words appearing in the text in bold, **like this**, are explained in the glossary.

A career in **leisure** and **tourism** – travel the world, meet people, have fun doing your favourite leisure activity – sounds like the perfect job, doesn't it? But is this really what it involves? Finding all the information to help you decide if this is the career for you can be difficult. That is where this book comes in. It will give you an introduction to what the leisure and tourism industry is and the sorts of jobs it offers. It will help you to work out if you would like to work in this industry. It will also show you that there is a lot more to the leisure and tourism industry than you might think!

It is very important to find the career that suits you so that you will be happy in your job. To find the perfect career needs a lot of careful thought and planning. This book aims to help you make the right decision.

YOUR CAREER ADVISOR

This book cannot tell you everything about the leisure and tourism industry, it can only give you an introduction. To find out about the organizations that interest you, you will need to visit their websites or write to them. You can also get more advice from your careers advisor at school. He or she will be able to help you choose the right career.

above: *A career in the leisure and tourism industry could mean your job is also your hobby!*

What do you imagine when you think of leisure and tourism? Do you picture the noisy swimming pool at your local leisure centre, or a **holiday representative** trying to get children to join in the fun and games? These are just two of hundreds of different types of careers in the huge and varied leisure and tourism industry.

A booming industry

The leisure and tourism industry is a huge **growth industry**, estimated to be worth £64 billion per year in the United Kingdom. Maybe that is why you think you would like to join the 2 million other people already employed in this industry. What's more, the industry is constantly expanding, which means more jobs will be available for you!

The reason for this growth is that today, people have more leisure time and more money to spend than at any other time in history. People are also living longer, and **retired** people have plenty of leisure time. There is a greater interest in keeping fit and healthy. People are taking short breaks and holidays in ever increasing numbers, and more and more overseas tourists are visiting the UK.

All this means an increasing number of jobs within the leisure and tourism industry. The future for the industry is bright. It is a great area to be considering for a career.

below: *Tourism is becoming a huge industry in the UK.*

Chapter 1

What is the leisure and tourism industry?

Before you go any further, let's think clearly about what leisure and tourism actually are. Your leisure time is the time when you are not at school or at work. It is the time when you are doing activities. Are you a member of a sports team? Have you been to the cinema or a museum recently? These are all examples of leisure activities.

During leisure time, people often travel away from home. When was the last time you went on holiday? Maybe you have been on a sightseeing tour of a European city recently? These are examples of tourism.

Working in leisure and tourism

The leisure and tourism industry provides the **facilities** and **services** that allow people to enjoy their leisure time. The range of careers is immense. Employers include:

◎ large leisure companies
◎ tour operators
◎ tourist boards
◎ local authorities
◎ leisure centres
◎ hotels
◎ sports clubs.

Get ahead!

Think about how you spend your leisure time. Write down all the leisure activities that you take part in during 1 week. Don't forget to include things like reading and watching television, as well as your more energetic activities.

What do you think it would be like to actually work in the leisure and tourism industry? The leisure and tourism industry is so huge, it can be divided into a number of sectors. These are described in this chapter. As you read through, think about whether some sectors appeal to you more than the others do.

Entertainment and visitor attractions

Entertainment and visitor attractions are at the very heart of the leisure and tourism industry. The UK has almost 6,500 visitor attractions, including historic buildings, theme parks, zoos, gardens, museums, and galleries. Around 135 million people go to the cinema each year, and even more visit museums. Entertainment venues and attractions act as a major draw for UK and overseas visitors, and they provide a large number of jobs for those interested in working in this industry.

Countryside recreation

The countryside is known as the great outdoors, and it is certainly very popular with lots of people in the UK. You only have to take a trip to the Lake District on a summer weekend to see this for yourself. The most popular countryside activities in the UK include walking and cycling. This sector provides 380,000 jobs, and the careers you can follow here are many and varied, from working with people to working with animals and plants.

Health and fitness

This is the fastest-growing area of the leisure and tourism industry and its popularity has doubled in the last 5 years. Gym membership has never been higher and over half a million people work in health and fitness in the UK. Many people want to become fitter and lead healthier lives, and the Government is trying to encourage people to take up more exercise.

below: *Yoga is a popular activity and yoga instructors are in great demand!*

While relatively few people earn a living from playing sport (not everyone can be David Beckham or Ellen MacArthur!), millions of people enjoy taking part in sport. Most people need the help of **coaches** and instructors, and make use of sports facilities and leisure centres. There are around 150,000 sports clubs in the UK, catering for all sports from aerobics to yachting. This adds up to a huge number of jobs.

Get ahead!

Visit the website of your local council. Look for all the leisure facilities available in your local area and list them. Think about the kinds of people who would use them and whether you would like to work in any of them.

Travel agents

A travel agency may either be one of a chain of shops or a single shop. Travel agents arrange holidays for people, usually through various tour operators (see opposite), so the customer has a lot of choice. At a travel agency people can book flights, accommodation, train tickets, and coach tickets. They can also book package deals, where the accommodation and flight are included in the price.

Most travel agents also provide information on the country you are visiting, such as whether you need any injections or what the weather will be like. They can also sell you **currency** for your holiday. In the larger agencies the work is often split into different divisions, for example, counter services, business travel, and **foreign exchange**. In smaller companies each member of staff will have to deal with all aspects of the agency's business.

below: *Travel agents try to offer you the best deal for a whole range of holidays.*

Tour operators

Tour operators create package holidays within the UK and abroad, including transport, accommodation, entertainment, and tour arrangements. They publish the details in holiday brochures so that travel agents can sell them to the public. Tour operators are similar to travel agents in that they provide holidays, but they only offer their own services, so cannot provide holidays created by other tour operators.

Tourist information and guiding services

Tourist information centres are found in almost every town in the UK. They are important for visitors as they provide lots of information on the local area such as maps, places of interest to visit, and details of any events.

Many travel companies provide guiding services on coach trips to inform the passengers about the area they are travelling through. In major cities you will find many different types of guiding services on offer. These range from open top buses to walking tours, to tours around **stately homes** and ancient buildings.

In this chapter you have looked at the main areas of the leisure and tourism industry. You will now go on to look at specific jobs that you could do within this diverse industry.

below: *The Tower of London is a hugely popular tourist attraction. Tour guides in historical buildings such as this often dress up in period costumes.*

Get ahead!

Visit your local tourist information centre and collect a range of leaflets suitable for a day visitor who wants to go sightseeing.

Chapter 2

What types of jobs are available?

The leisure and tourism industry offers a huge range of jobs, from working in your local park to entertaining guests on a huge cruise liner. Most jobs are concerned with helping people to enjoy their leisure time. Some jobs involve very active work whereas some are desk-bound. Opportunities for work exist throughout the UK, and there are jobs at all levels – management, professional, skilled, and semi-skilled. Every job is different and everyone has different expectations about what they want to achieve in their career.

Read through the following jobs and try to decide if any of them appeal to you. If they don't, this does not mean a career in the leisure and tourism industry is not for you. This is just a small selection of the vast array of jobs that exist within the industry.

Tour guide

A tour guide shows UK and overseas visitors around tourist sites such as cities, museums, historic buildings, or gardens. You will do this either on foot or by transport such as a coach or river boat tour. As a tour guide, you will also make presentations explaining, for example, the history of an area or site. You will also need to be prepared to answer any questions people may have and help with any difficulties.

left *Tour guides must be careful not to lose any of their clients!*

Leisure centre manager

A leisure centre manager is responsible for the overall organization of a leisure centre. Your main duties will involve dealing with staff. You will need to decide how many people you need to employ, then interview and train them. You will also be responsible for your employees' safety while at work. Other duties may include deciding what equipment to buy or replace, planning the best use of the annual **budget**, and dealing with a whole range of problems such as complaints, troublemakers, and blocked toilets.

Health and fitness instructor

A health and fitness instructor works in a gym or leisure centre and organizes exercise programmes for individuals. Instructors also lead groups in a range of activities including aerobics, weight training, circuit training, aquarobics, and step. Every leisure centre and gym needs instructors, so there are plenty of jobs, particularly in private clubs. Up to 4,500 fitness centres and clubs around the UK employ around 50,000 people, and the number is increasing. Even though the fitness industry is growing there is still strong competition for jobs.

As a health and fitness instructor your job will involve planning exercise programmes, making up exercise routines set to music, and leading classes. It will also involve demonstrating the safe use of gym equipment and correct exercise techniques, as well as making sure that people do not suffer injury through incorrect

Get ahead!

Find out about three more jobs in the leisure and tourism industry and list the main duties for each.

or excessive exercise. You may also design personal workout programmes and you may be expected to give advice on **nutrition** and lifestyle.

Ground staff

Ground staff work at sports grounds, for example, cricket, rugby or football pitches, or golf courses. The main area of work you would be involved in is ensuring the pitch or course is in good condition for those who use it.

Get ahead!

List any sporting venues you know of in the following categories:
• cricket
• rugby
• golf.
Write to one of them, asking for information on the type of work that ground staff are likely to undertake.

Park warden

The job of a park warden is to manage all aspects of a park. This could be a town or city park, a country park, or a larger area of wilderness such as a **national park**. It is a very varied job and your duties could include dealing with litter and damage to plants, repairing fencing, and general **conservation** work. You will also be expected to educate the public, by giving presentations, guided nature walks, answering questions, and dealing with any problems. Problems may involve people who are lost, injuries, and troublemakers. You are also responsible for the safety of the visitors while they are in the park.

below: *Working as a member of the ground staff team means you get to take advantage of working outdoors in the sunshine.*

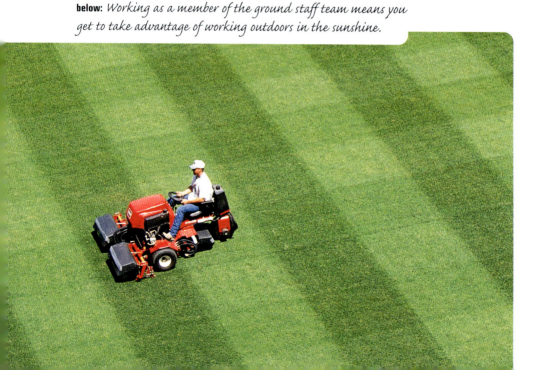

Pool attendant

Every public swimming pool in the UK needs a pool attendant, or lifeguard, to look after the safety of the people using the pool and rescue anyone who gets into difficulty. As a pool attendant it is your job to prevent accidents, so you must be constantly alert to danger and ready to help any swimmer in difficulty. Duties would include:

- ◎ observing swimmers, especially young children and weak swimmers
- ◎ dealing with minor accidents such as people slipping on wet surfaces
- ◎ dealing with troublemakers
- ◎ cleaning the pool area.

In an emergency situation you may need to jump into the pool to rescue someone, and then give first aid treatment to the casualty.

Travel consultant

A travel consultant works in a travel agency and advises customers about travel arrangements within the UK or abroad. This may involve putting together a package of travel, accommodation, car hire, and **travel insurance** to suit the customer's needs. It may also involve selling airline tickets for travel, making hotel bookings, taking payments from the public, and giving advice on types of holidays, methods of travel, **passports**, **vaccinations**, and foreign currency. In order to do this, you need to have a good knowledge of all the products offered by all the tour operators.

Get ahead!

Look into doing a lifeguard qualification. Go to the Royal Lifesaving Society (RLSS) website at www.lifesavers.org.uk/ or www.lifeguardskills.co.uk/ to find out about relevant courses, qualifications, and training.

Resort representative

A resort representative or "rep" looks after groups of holidaymakers, usually abroad, including organizing trips and dealing with problems. This gives you the opportunity to meet lots of people and live in interesting places. You are also responsible for the safety of the holidaymakers in your care.

As a resort rep your main duties will include some or all of the following: meeting the holidaymakers at the airport; helping them to get their accommodation; and organizing a welcome meeting at their hotel to provide them with information on the local area. You may also need to help holidaymakers with any problems during their stay, for example, if someone loses their passport or becomes ill. Many reps work with children and will organize children's activities and **crèches**.

below: As a resort rep (see centre, wearing green) you will have the opportunity to work in many different locations and you will meet many different people.

above: *Tourist information offices are the starting point for many visitors to a city.*

Tourist information centre assistant

A tourist information centre assistant provides information about the local area, either by answering customer's queries face to face in the office, or by telephone or email. You may be asked for directions to a certain place or suggestions for what to do, so you need to know the area well. You may also be asked to find and book accommodation or concert tickets for visiting tourists.

Cinema attendant

Cinema attendants, also known as ushers, work in cinemas. They sell tickets and refreshments, show members of the audience to their seats, and clean up after the show. Other duties include checking tickets, selling programmes, and usually answering telephone enquiries.

As an usher you are responsible for making sure that audiences behave properly and are safe. You would be expected to supervise the **cinema auditorium** during the performance. You would have to stop people from blocking fire exits and, in the event of an emergency, supervise people leaving the cinema building.

In this chapter you have looked at just a few of the many and varied jobs in the leisure and tourism industry. In the next chapter you will move on to look at what you can expect your working environment to be like should you work in the leisure and tourism industry.

Chapter 3

What will the working environment be like?

Are you an outdoors person or do you prefer to work indoors? Do you like to know what you have to do each day or do you like surprises? In this chapter you will begin to get an idea of the working environment you can expect for jobs in the leisure and tourism industry.

WHAT DO YOU WANT FROM YOUR CAREER?

You need to think about you career choice carefully. Different people want different things from their careers. You may want:

- a challenge
- a lot of money
- the security of having a job
- a chance to develop your skills
- the opportunity to travel
- job satisfaction
- flexibility
- the oppotunity to make a difference to people's lives.

Many people try to work in the leisure and tourism industry because "they want to travel". While some jobs may give you the opportunity to do this, the reality is that you will spend much of your time indoors rather than on the beach. The work is certainly not always as exciting as it may sound. You may well be living in a glamorous location, but jobs in the leisure and tourism industry often involve long hours, hard work, and limited pay.

Get ahead!

List the things you want from your career. Now list the type of work that interests you. Finally, list the things you definitely don't want to do. Do you think a career in the leisure and tourism industry might be for you?

Working conditions

Working conditions vary. Some jobs are indoors, for example, in an office, shop, gym, sports hall, or cinema. Others are largely outdoors, for example, in gardens or parks. Some have a mix of the two, particularly in tourism. Holiday reps and tour guides, for example, work both indoors and outdoors.

Mental and physical demands

If you work in a travel agency or tourist information centre, you will be in the office all day. You will either be dealing with customers face to face or indirectly over the phone or by email. Much of your work will involve using a computer. The work can be stressful as there might be queues of people all wanting your attention at busy times.

Many jobs in the leisure and tourism industry can be physically demanding. As a health and fitness instructor, for example, you will be actively taking part in exercise classes for a large part of the day. A number of jobs, including pool attendant, tour guide, and holiday rep, will require you to be on your feet for most of the day. In addition, if you work as a pool attendant, the atmosphere will be **humid** and stuffy, and if you work in a leisure centre it is likely to be very noisy during the school holidays and at weekends.

below: *If you chose a career that involves lots of outdoor work, you may end up working in all sorts of weather conditions!*

Emotional demands

The work can also be emotionally demanding, as, for most jobs involving dealing with people, you must appear enthusiastic all the time. In particular, if you work as a tour guide you may have to wear historical costume or carry something such as a colourful umbrella to help the group see you in the crowds. You may find this embarrassing at first, but it is a necessary part of the job and you will need to grin and bear it.

Seasonal work

Work in the tourism sector is often **seasonal**. This means you may not be needed to work at all times of the year. A **chalet** host in a ski resort, for example, will only be needed during the winter, whereas a children's rep on a campsite in France will only be needed for the summer. A tour guide may also only be needed during the summer months, when tourists visit a city.

Get ahead!

Visit www.totaljobs.com and search for jobs under the headings "leisure" and "tourism". Are there any you would like to do?

CASE STUDY

Paul works as a seasonal receptionist at a campsite in the Lake District.

I only have this job for the summer, because not many people come camping in the winter. I spend most of my time in the small shed that is our office, mainly dealing with arrivals and answering people's questions. I work long hours, about 10 hours a day, but I need the money, and the job only lasts from April until September. During the winter I work as a chalet host in different ski resorts in Europe. This involves cleaning the chalet and cooking meals for the guests. I get time off during the day when I can go skiing myself, but I am usually so tired I end up catching up on sleep.

Travelling with your job

There may be a lot of travel involved in some tourism-related jobs. Tour guides may need to travel with the people they are guiding; this may include staying away from home overnight. A holiday rep will be required to live at the resort, so will be away from friends and family for months at a time. This may make you feel **isolated**, especially if you have to learn a new **culture** and language on the job.

A typical working day?

In general in the leisure and tourism industry, you will not have a typical working day. Many jobs involve working very long hours, including

above: *Working in the leisure and tourism industry may take you to some fabulous locations.*

mornings, evenings, nights, and weekends. If you work as a holiday rep you may even be **on call** 24 hours a day. This means that you have to help holidaymakers in the middle of the night or at any other time they need you. As a tour guide you can expect to work 40–60 hours a week during the tourist season, but you might not work at all during the winter months. If you work in a cinema you will work mostly in the afternoons and evenings until about midnight.

The best people to tell you about a typical working day in the leisure and tourism industry are those who work in it. Some examples are shown on the following pages.

Jasmine works as a **freelance** aerobics instructor.

As I am freelance I work in lots of different places – leisure centres, private gyms, university sports centres, and many more. I have to work out my timetable of teaching carefully, as obviously I need to travel between the different venues. The busiest times are lunchtimes and evenings. All this running around, together with taking the classes, means that I need lots of energy for my job.

Andrew works as a freelance tour guide in Edinburgh.

I normally work from 9.00 a.m. to 6.00 p.m., but this can vary a lot. I will work much fewer hours in winter. Some days start with an open-top bus tour of the city, during which I provide commentary through a microphone. I also work some evenings, taking people on ghost tours and evening walks. I work freelance, so my work tends to vary a lot.

Dylan works as a rep at a beach resort in Spain.

Every day my job is different. My usual hours are 8.30 a.m. to 12.30 p.m. and then 4.30 p.m. to 8.00 p.m. Sometimes my day begins much earlier if I have to take guests who are leaving for the airport. I would then stay at the airport and spend the morning meeting new guests as they arrive and helping them find the right bus to their hotels. I spend most days dealing with customers. I could be doing anything from answering their questions to coping with minor injuries to dealing with complaints. I tend to work long hours but you get used to coping without much sleep.

Saskia works as an assistant manager at a private health club.

*My day will be spent showing new members around the gym, organizing the team of 30 staff, and doing lots of **administration** work. Things always happen unexpectedly, so I have to be prepared for anything. This means I have a lot of variety in my job, which I enjoy. I work shifts, so some days I start at 5.00 a.m., but then I finish at 3.00 p.m. Working late shifts plays havoc with my social life, but I just have to plan things in advance.*

In contrast, if you work in a travel agency or tourist information office you will have set hours. You will usually be expected to work shop hours, which are mainly 9.00 a.m. to 5.00 p.m., Monday to Friday. In addition, you may have to work some weekends.

How much will I get paid?

For some people, this is the most important question when deciding on a career. If you are one of these people, then maybe the leisure and tourism industry is not for you. **Salaries** are often low for these types of jobs, although there may be other **perks** such as cheap travel or living expenses. However, if money comes secondary to enjoying what you do and making people happy, then you are in the right place.

below: *Salaries in the leisure and tourism industry are often low.*

Rates of pay very a lot in the leisure and tourism industry, depending on your specific job, where you work, the size of the company, your experience and your qualifications. Some examples are given below.

◎ Holiday reps can earn between £10,000 and £18,000 a year, usually including free accommodation, food, and travel.
◎ Tour guides can earn between £6,000 and £25,000, but most are self-employed, and earnings vary hugely depending on the number of hours worked.
◎ Travel consultants can earn from around £8,000 to £20,000 a year. Some companies pay **commission** on any holidays you sell. You may also get discounts on holiday packages you buy.
◎ As a health and fitness instructor your starting pay might be around £12,000 a year. This can rise to £25,000 with experience.
◎ A pool attendant can expect to earn around £12,000 per year, but most are employed as and when they are needed and will earn less.
◎ As a sports or leisure centre manager your starting salary could be in the range of £15,000 per year, rising with experience to around £25,000 a year.
◎ As a cinema attendant your earnings will range from £8,000 to £12,000. Many posts are part-time.

CASE STUDY

Jenny works as a countryside warden in Northumberland.

I didn't get into this career until later in life. I did a degree in Geography as I've always been interested in the natural landscape. I then had to work as a voluntary leader on conservation holidays before I could get a paid job, so I would advise not going into conservation if you want to make a lot of money.

*There is no such thing as a typical day. Most mornings I walk around the park, check fishing **permits**, collect litter, and replace broken fences. In the afternoon I may lead a guided walk and help visitors by giving general advice and answering questions. At any time I may also need to deal with wrongdoers trying to damage the park property.*

Chapter 4

Am I the right person for the job?

As you will know by now, there are many different types of jobs in the leisure and tourism industry, so it is difficult to pinpoint one set of skills that you will need whatever job you are applying for. You will find there are opportunities for many different types of people. In this section you will look at the main personal qualities and skills that might be useful for jobs in this industry.

Get ahead!

As you read the information in this chapter, think carefully about your own personality and your likes and dislikes.

People skills and enthusiasm

You need to enjoy working with people for all jobs in the leisure and tourism industry. So, ask yourself this question now: do I really enjoy working with people? Leisure and tourism might not be everyone's choice, but if the answer to this question is "yes", it might well be for you.

You need to be self-confident and enthusiastic at all times, even when you are tired and miserable. You must always appear happy and smiling to the people you work with. After all, if you were on holiday you would not be very impressed if your holiday rep or tour guide looked bored all week.

left: *Even though you may be feeling tired, as a fitness instructor you will have to make yourself seem full of energy.*

As a fitness instructor you will have to **motivate** the whole class and you cannot do this without injecting a lot of enthusiasm into your workout. It is sometimes difficult to be enthusiastic all the time, so you also need a lot of stamina and to stay active and lively, even when you are tired.

CASE STUDY

Radika works as a fitness class instructor.

*I am self-employed, which is great as it means I get to choose the hours I work. I do a mixture of Body Pump, Body Combat, and Circuit Training classes. In my line of work it helps if you are a bit of a performer, as you need to inspire and motivate people to do the best they can. I get quite frustrated sometimes when I think people are being a bit lazy, but I have to be **tolerant** and never show my frustration to them. I also need a lot of energy to take three or four classes a day, and it helps to have a good sense of rhythm, so you don't get lost in the middle of a class.*

Communication skills

To work in the leisure and tourism industry, you need to have excellent communication skills. If you are speaking to a large group of people at a welcome meeting in a resort or on a tour bus, for example, you need to speak clearly so that everyone can hear you. Ability with modern foreign languages will also be useful, for example, French, Spanish, German, or Italian, so you can explain things to foreign visitors in their own language if necessary.

left: *Many tourists will be overseas visitors, so if you can speak other languages you will be at a great advantage.*

CASE STUDY

Gavin works as a holiday rep in a resort in Greece.

Part of my job is to organize welcome presentations for the holidaymakers when they arrive. There can be up to 40 people in the room, all wanting to get on with their holiday and not listen to me. I found it very difficult and embarrassing at first, as I have to try to get their attention and keep it while I tell them about the resort and the tours they can go on. Now I have done it a few times I feel much more confident, and my presentation skills have improved enormously.

As well as people from the UK, we get many holidaymakers from France, Italy, and Germany. Foreign language skills are therefore very important. I speak French and German fluently, and can get by in Spanish and Italian. I enjoy speaking in different languages, and I can see that the visitors really appreciate it when someone speaks their language.

CASE STUDY

Tahmina works as a reservation assistant for a tour operator.

As most of my time is spent dealing with customers over the phone, the main skill you need for this job is a good telephone manner. I also need to be able to listen very carefully, so that I understand exactly what the customer wants. It would also be useful to have IT skills, but I received lots of training in this when I started.

Dealing with the public

As you will be dealing with the public a lot of the time, you should have a smart appearance. You also need to be friendly and approachable as, for many jobs in the leisure and tourism industry, you will be expected to help people, provide them with information, and answer their questions.

Adaptability

In the leisure and tourism industry, you will also need to be flexible and adaptable, as your job may be constantly changing. Sometimes you may need to deal with emergencies and you will have to remain calm under pressure. A pool attendant will need to remain alert, for example, even though there may be distractions. You will also need to keep calm when dealing with complaining customers. Would you be able to keep your cool when dealing with an angry customer who blamed you for the fact that he or she did not enjoy a holiday or visit to the museum? You need a lot of patience and tolerance to cope effectively in this situation.

below: *Would you have a cool enough head to be able to deal with emergency situations?*

Other skills

There are also some more specific skills that you need for certain jobs within the leisure and tourism industries.

◉ For jobs in the health and fitness sector, as well as tour guides, you need to be physically fit.

◉ As a tour guide you also need to have a good memory and know your facts about the tour area well, so you are able to answer any questions the tourists may have.

◉ For office-based jobs you will need good keyboard and IT skills.

◉ Travel consultants need to be well organized with good research skills to enable them to create the ideal holiday package for customers.

◉ If you are working in a leisure centre or as park warden you will need assertiveness for dealing firmly with rowdy or difficult people.

◉ As manager of a leisure centre you will need good business sense and organizational skills.

above: *If you work with children you will need a lot of patience and a caring nature.*

Teamworking skills

In most jobs in the leisure and tourism industry you will work as part of a team. Therefore, you do not need to have all of the skills mentioned above, but it is important that you can contribute a lot of them to your team. Sometimes, however, you will be expected to work on your own, and at times you will need to use your **initiative** to make decisions.

Finding the right job for you

Finding the best career for you involves matching your personality and skills to the skills needed for a particular job. The best way to do this is to start by taking a close look at yourself.

◎ Are you confident and outgoing?
◎ Are your communication skills strong?
◎ Do you cope well under pressure?
◎ Do you enjoy working with children?

It is unlikely that you would enjoy working as a children's holiday rep on a campsite in Italy if you can't stand the idea of having to cope with screaming children, don't speak Italian, and can think of nothing worse than living in a tent for half the year.

SKILLS CHECKLIST

Copy out and fill in the checklist of skills below. Look back at the information in this chapter to see if your skills match up with those required by jobs in the leisure and tourism industry. Can you identify any area of the industry that you are particularly suited to?

Skills required	Yes (✔)	No (✔)	Especially important for:
Enjoy working with people	☐	☐	All leisure and tourism jobs
Self-confident	☐	☐	Holiday representative
Enthusiastic	☐	☐	Fitness instructor
Good communication skills	☐	☐	All leisure and tourism jobs
Friendly	☐	☐	All leisure and tourism jobs
Approachable	☐	☐	Holiday representative
Adaptable	☐	☐	All leisure and tourism jobs
Able to deal with emergencies	☐	☐	Pool attendant
Able to remain calm under pressure	☐	☐	Pool attendant
Work well in a team	☐	☐	All leisure and tourism jobs

Chapter 5

What qualifications do I need?

Now you know what kind of person would be best suited to working in the leisure and tourism industry, but what qualifications do you need?

above: *Studying for a qualification in a leisure and tourism related subject can help you progress in your career.*

While some jobs demand particular qualifications for entry, for example, working as a pool attendant, many do not. In general, most of the jobs in this industry have no set entry requirements. Much of the training for jobs is provided on the job. It is therefore possible to find a job in the leisure and tourism industry without any qualifications. However, jobs in the leisure and tourism industry are popular and competition can be tough, so it can be useful to gain a relevant qualification.

Why study for a qualification?

By gaining a recognized qualification you are likely to have a much wider range of career opportunities and better chances of **promotion**. Many qualifications can help prepare you for entry to leisure and tourism jobs, from GCSEs, **National Vocational Qualifications** (NVQs)/**Scottish Vocational Qualifications** (SVQs), and **apprenticeships**, through to degrees and postgraduate qualifications. You need to think about what you want to do within the industry, then you can decide which qualifications are most suitable.

Chris has his own business letting holiday properties in North Wales.

*I have a **Masters** degree in Tourism Management, but it was more the management side of the degree that has helped me rather than the tourism aspect. I really got into letting houses through taking opportunities rather than using the qualifications I have. My old next-door neighbour was having trouble getting a long-term let for her house, so I rented it from her and then **sublet** it on a weekly basis. The rest of my business came through word of mouth.*

above: *There are many different courses and qualifications that are relevant for working in the leisure and tourism industry.*

For the jobs given below, there is no single entry route. The qualifications described are the most common and most relevant for the particular job, but are by no means the only qualifications you could consider.

Holiday representative

There are no set qualifications needed for the job of a holiday rep, but employers may prefer applicants with GCSEs (grades A–C) or S-grades (grades 1–3) in English, Maths, Geography, ICT, and Foreign Languages. Relevant NVQs/SVQs that you could consider include Outdoor Education, Development Training, and Recreation and Playwork Levels 2 and 3. Travel and Tourism HND or degree courses may provide a useful background.

Tour guide

Guides do not need qualifications, but a good general education is required, particularly a knowledge of history or the area where you will be working. Most guides in the UK train for the **Blue Badge qualification**. Training for this is part-time and lasts between 6 months and 2 years. Entry depends on skills and experience rather than academic qualifications, but the training is demanding, and you need to put aside a lot of time to complete it.

There are also relevant NVQs/SVQs that you could gain such as Tourist Information Services Levels 2 and 3, Heritage Care and Visitor Services Level 2, and Cultural Heritage Operations Level 3.

Travel consultant

No formal qualification is required to work as a travel consultant, but most employers look for a good standard of secondary education, including GCSEs (grades A–C) or S-grades (grades 1–3) in English, Maths, Geography, and Foreign Languages. A GCSE in ICT would also be useful.

WHICH QUALIFICATION?

◉ NVQs/SVQs: These are more practical and less academic than A-levels. They provide a flexible approach to studying a number of different subjects and allow you to progress at your own pace. They have been developed to prepare you for a variety of jobs. You can gain NVQs/SVQs by taking a full-time course at college or you can study part-time while at work.

◉ **Modern Apprenticeships**: These provide an opportunity to develop skills and expertise and gain NVQs/SVQs while at work. Organizations such as the Travel Training Company run Modern Apprenticeship schemes.

◉ Further and Higher Education: Many universities and some colleges offer **Higher National Certificate** (HNC), **Higher National Diploma** (HND), or degree courses in Leisure and Tourism and other related subject areas. Often these courses include business studies, field trips, foreign languages, and marketing elements. You can also do sandwich degrees, where you spend 1 year working in industry. These are popular with employers, as they know you will have a large amount of work experience.

◉ Specialist qualifications: Some organizations within the leisure and tourism industry offer their own qualifications. These include the ABTA Travel Agent's Certificate and the ABTA Tour Operators' Certificate. (ABTA stands for Association of British Travel Agents.)

The most common way of starting work in a travel agents is through a Modern Apprenticeship scheme. The Travel Training Company operates a Travel Training Programme. This involves work experience and training and leads to NVQ/SVQ Levels 2 and 3 in Travel Services. The following qualifications would also be relevant:

◎ ABTA Travel Agents Certificate (ABTAC)
◎ A-level/Higher in Travel and Tourism
◎ HNC/HND in Tourism or Travel and Tourism
◎ Degree in Travel and Tourism or a related field such as Business Studies or Finance (with Tourism options).

CASE STUDY

Winston is training to be a travel consultant for a travel agency.

I applied to do a Modern Apprenticeship after talking to my careers advisor at school. It's a good way to get qualifications, because I am earning money at the same time. In the mornings I work on my NVQ in Travel Services and in the afternoons I deal with customers. The other staff at the travel agency help me a lot, and all my training is on the job.

Health and fitness instructor

To be a health and fitness instructor, no academic qualifications are needed. However, it is necessary to obtain a specialist qualification, for example, the Fitness Exercise Teaching Certificate (or equivalent), which may be done full-time or part-time. This includes a written test on **anatomy**, exercise techniques, and nutrition, and a practical test on teaching a class. Once you have this qualification you need to get your name on the Register of Exercise Professionals. This demonstrates your professional status to employers.

To be a health and fitness instructor, you could:

◎ study full-time for NVQs/SVQs in Fitness, Health and Exercise, Coaching, Teaching and Instructing, and related subjects
◎ study similar subjects full-time at a higher level, such as an HNC, HND, or degree courses in Fitness, Health and Exercise, Sports Science, and related subjects
◎ study part-time through organizations such as the **Young Men's Christian Association** (YMCA).

Pool attendant

To work as a pool attendant it is necessary to hold the Royal Life Saving Society (RLSS) National Pool Lifeguard Certificate, which you will need to renew every 3 years. You can work towards this qualification at evening classes at most swimming pools. If your duties include water quality maintenance, you can do a foundation module from the Institute of Sport and Recreation Management (ISRM), which leads to the National Pool Plant Operators' Certificate.

Get ahead!

Find out where you can do a lifesaving certificate in your local area.

No educational qualifications are required to become a pool attendant, but many employers expect GCSEs in English and Maths. In addition to a lifesaving certificate, a general first aid qualification would also be extremely useful.

right: *Swimming is a skill for life and good swimming instructors are in high demand.*

Imran worked as a pool attendant for many years before becoming a swimming teacher.

My career in sport began when I was a competitive swimmer. When I was 18, I gained my National Pool Lifeguard Certificate and got a job as a pool attendant at my local leisure centre. I worked full-time for 5 years, but started training part-time for my Amateur Swimming Association (ASA) Assistant Swim Teacher's Certificate. I helped with swimming lessons at a nearby pool and once I had enough experience I gained my ASA Swim Teacher's Certificate. I've now been a swimming instructor for 6 months and love it.

Leisure centre manager

There are no set requirements, but the following qualifications would be helpful (apprenticeships may also be available):

◎ NVQ/SVQ in Sports and Recreation or a similar subject
◎ HNC/HND in a Sports or Leisure Management related subject
◎ Degree in Sports or Leisure Management
◎ Degree in any subject, plus a postgraduate qualification in Leisure Management.

Cinema attendant

You do not need formal qualifications, but should be able to use a computer and handle cash. Some experience of dealing with people, for example, as a shop assistant, would also be useful.

Cinemas are usually owned and operated by large leisure groups, which may offer opportunities for formal training. You will learn on the job, with supervision from experienced staff.

One thing you should note is that qualifications alone are no guarantee of a job in the leisure and tourism industry. A lot depends on your personality, attitude, communication skills, and common-sense approach to work and life in general.

Get ahead!

Find a copy of a local newspaper. Identify as many jobs in leisure and tourism as you can. For each job list the skills and qualifications you need.

Chapter 6

A foot in the door

You enjoy working with people and have excellent communication skills. You seem like the ideal candidate for a position in the leisure and tourism industry . . . but how do you set about actually getting a job?

Do well at school

Whatever job you are applying for in the leisure and tourism industry, most employers look for a good standard of secondary education, including GCSEs (grades A–C) or S-grades (grades 1–3) in English, Maths, and foreign languages.

Your Maths and English skills will be important in any job that you do. Most jobs in the leisure and tourism industry will require you to take payments from customers. Your Maths skills will be useful for dealing with cash, cheques, and card transactions. You may also become involved in ordering items that you need, for example, weights for a leisure centre or leaflets for tourists. In addition you may be given responsibility for managing part of the budget, so you need to be competent with numbers.

Good English skills will be needed for writing formal letters, reports, and sending information round to work colleagues by email. If you have to speak to groups as part of your job, your oral presentation skills also need to be good. Other subjects, such as History and Business Studies, will give you useful communication skills as well.

right: *Make sure you spend your time at school wisely!*

above: *As a tour guide you will need to be confident in speaking to large groups of people.*

DRAMATIC IMPACT

Drama can be useful for a lot of jobs in the leisure and tourism industry, as you need to be confident and outgoing. It can help you to build your confidence and put more expression into your presentations.

Foreign languages such as French, German, Spanish, or Italian are obviously very useful, and sometimes necessary for jobs in the tourism sector. If you are a rep living in one of these countries you will be required to speak the language. It is also useful for tour guides working in the UK to have some ability with languages, so they can conduct tours in a foreign language if required.

A good knowledge of geography, especially a knowledge of where places are, can be very helpful in the tourism industry, and being good at sport is necessary for many of the jobs based in gyms and leisure centres.

Work experience

You may find that a relevant qualification will help your employment prospects. However, the key factor employers will be looking for is relevant experience, especially of working with the public. Relevant work experience can therefore be very important and you should try to gain some before applying for jobs. Luckily, work experience opportunities are plentiful. Holiday work is available at peak times and **casual work** is available all year round.

The job for you?

Not only is work experience important for impressing employers, it also gives you the chance to find out if this is actually what you want to do as a career. Any work experience, whether it is a placement organized by your school or part-time work you have organized yourself, will give you an idea of what the job itself is like and the realities of working life.

Making the most of your work experience

Once you have completed your work experience, you should think about what you got out of it and make a note of this. Describe any new skills or experiences that you gained such as dealing with customers, working in a team, or making presentations. You could give an oral presentation or a written report about your work experience to your class, and in this way gain useful communication skills.

What work experience should I do?

There are plenty of things you can do while you are still at school or college that could improve your chances of getting into your chosen career. Some of these are described below.

Park warden

Voluntary work experience is often necessary before you will be considered for a job. However, there are many ways you can do practical conservation work as a **volunteer**. You could offer to help at weekends in your local park, you could go on a **National Trust** working holiday, or you could work as a volunteer with the British Trust for Conservation Volunteers.

above: *Working as a volunteer for organizations, such as the British Trust for Conservation Volunteers, offers excellent work experience.*

Holiday rep

It would be useful to gain experience of working with young people and children, for example, in a play scheme or youth club. Experience of dealing with large groups would also be advantageous and, again, a youth club would be a good place to start.

Experience of living or travelling overseas is also looked on favourably by employers. You could think about working as a volunteer on a **kibbutz** in Israel or a campsite in France during your summer holiday.

Tourist information centre

It would be helpful to gain some experience of working with customers. You could work in a shop, where you will be communicating with a range of people. You will also gain confidence in dealing with the general public face to face, which will help you to deal with any questions or problems that could arise as a tourist information assistant.

Sports coach

You could volunteer to coach your sport at a school or local sports club. If you are interested in coaching swimming you could volunteer to help at your local leisure centre or swimming club. You can work towards an ASA Helpers Certificate to prove to employers that you have the experience. This is also a good way to gain experience of working with people.

How to stand out from the crowd

Jobs in the leisure and tourism industry are seen as glamorous and are therefore very popular. There may be hundreds of enthusiastic young people competing for the same job as you. It is therefore not enough to have the relevant qualifications and work experience – you need to stand out from the crowd. Your skills and personality are more important than academic qualifications for many jobs in leisure and tourism, so think about what you have to offer.

USEFUL TO HAVE...

◎ A modern European language for jobs such as reps and tour guides.
◎ A driving licence is necessary for some jobs.
◎ A first aid qualification.

Applying for jobs

To discover what jobs are on offer in the leisure and tourism industry you can find information in a number of places.

◎ Look in newspapers, both local and national, for job adverts.

◎ Talk to your careers advisor at school.

◎ Visit the careers section of your local library.

◎ Look for the names of companies that you might be interested in working for on the Internet and in brochures. You can then write to them to see if they have any suitable work.

◎ Search the Internet for jobs. If you want to work in travel, for example, the Association of British Travel Agents (ABTA) website lists vacancies in the companies that are members of ABTA. If you want to work in a tourist information office a list of tourist information centres can be found on the Britain Express website.

◎ Visit job centres and recruitment agencies.

Some examples of the types of job vacancies you might see in your local paper are shown below.

Fitness Instructor
Salary: £15,000 per year

An energetic fitness instructor is required to work in a private health club. The applicant must have an outgoing personality and relevant qualifications.
Excellent career opportunities.

POOL ATTENDANT
Salary: £5 per hour

A responsible pool attendant is required for patrolling the pool during peak times, carrying out pool water tests and general cleaning duties.

Relevant qualifications are necessary.

Travel Consultant

An independent travel agency is looking for a hard working individual who can think on his or her feet and enjoys working with people. For the suitable candidate we offer a competitive salary, generous holiday allowance and good opportunities for training and travel.

When you apply for a job, you will either have to fill in an application form or provide a CV. Whichever method you use, this will be the first impression the employer gets of you, so you need to get it right.

Completing application forms

If the employer sends you an application form, then you must use this to apply for the job. The first thing you should do is photocopy the form, so you can create a rough draft on the photocopy. This way, if you make any mistakes, it does not matter.

Read through all the questions before you start, then take your time to fill in the answers. Make sure you answer the questions actually asked, and always be honest in your answers. If you make things up the chances are that you will get found out if you make it to the interview stage.

below: *Talk to your careers advisor to find out what jobs are available in the leisure and tourism industry.*

Before you fill your form in, it is very useful to try and work out what the employer will be looking for. Write down everything you think they will want to see evidence of on your application form. Then write down the skills you have that would be relevant to those required by the employer. They might be things you have done in school projects, your work experience, or one of your hobbies.

Once you have checked your form for spelling mistakes, grammar, and punctuation you can copy it on to the original application form.

Get ahead!

Copy out and fill in the application form below, using as many of the following phrases as possible. They are all things employers will like to see on your application form.
- Enthusiastic
- Hard working
- Good at writing and speaking clearly
- Honest
- Good at working in a team
- Reliable
- Willing to learn

Keep your writing neat and tidy and check the form again before sending it off – or better still, get someone else to check it for you. Make sure you post it well before the closing date, and use a suitable envelope. Do not fold your application form. Keep the photocopy in case you get an interview and need to check what you wrote.

Follow all the instructions on the form.

Make sure you begin with your most recent job or placement.

APPLICATION FORM
Please use black ink

Job title

PERSONAL DETAILS
First name
Surname
Date of birth
Address
Phone number
E-mail address
Post code

WORK EXPERIENCE
Begin with your most recent employment, but include any work experience or voluntary work.

| Employer's name | Your title | Dates of employment |
| | | From   To |

Include any part-time work you have done.

QUALIFICATIONS
Begin with your most recent qualifications.

| Subject/Course | Level (Standard, Higher, SVQ, Unit, Other) | Year taken | Final result |
| | | | |

PERSONAL PROFILE
Use this space to give any additional information that may be of interest to the employer.

Describe any relevant hobbies you may have.

State why you are interested in the job.

Include any relevant skills and experience that you have not already mentioned.

REFERENCE
Please provide the name and address of someone who can be asked for a reference.

| Name and job title | Address | Telephone number |

I confirm that the information on this form is true and correct to the best of my knowledge.

Signature
Date

41

CVs and covering letters

A curriculum vitae (CV) is a form that tells employers about your education, experience, and interests. Some employers will ask for a CV instead of sending you an application form to fill in. When you write your CV you will need to include all the information that the employer would have requested from you on an application form. You will also need to send a covering letter explaining why you are applying for the job.

An example of a good CV is shown below. As you can see, it has been typed and has a clear layout. It first gives your personal details, such as your name, address, and school. It then describes your qualifications, work experience, and interests. Do not try to include too much information on your CV as this will make it difficult to read. It should not be more than two pages long. Make sure all the spelling, grammar, and punctuation are correct, and ask someone if they would mind checking it before you send it off.

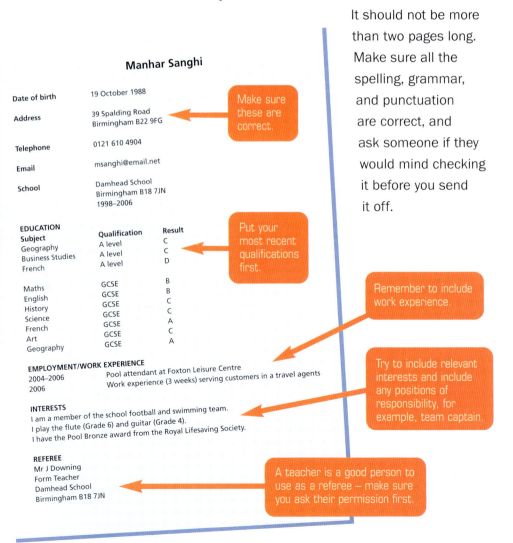

Manhar Sanghi

Date of birth	19 October 1988
Address	39 Spalding Road Birmingham B22 9FG
Telephone	0121 610 4904
Email	msanghi@email.net
School	Damhead School Birmingham B18 7JN 1998–2006

Make sure these are correct.

EDUCATION

Subject	Qualification	Result
Geography	A level	C
Business Studies	A level	C
French	A level	D
Maths	GCSE	B
English	GCSE	B
History	GCSE	C
Science	GCSE	C
French	GCSE	A
Art	GCSE	C
Geography	GCSE	A

Put your most recent qualifications first.

Remember to include work experience.

EMPLOYMENT/WORK EXPERIENCE
2004–2006   Pool attendant at Foxton Leisure Centre
2006   Work experience (3 weeks) serving customers in a travel agents

Try to include relevant interests and include any positions of responsibility, for example, team captain.

INTERESTS
I am a member of the school football and swimming team.
I play the flute (Grade 6) and guitar (Grade 4).
I have the Pool Bronze award from the Royal Lifesaving Society.

REFEREE
Mr J Downing
Form Teacher
Damhead School
Birmingham B18 7JN

A teacher is a good person to use as a referee – make sure you ask their permission first.

You should always send a handwritten or typed covering letter with your CV that explains why you are applying for the job. You need to make your covering letter specific to the job you are applying for.

Always address it to a specific person – never write "Dear Sir/Madam" (you may even need to contact the organization by telephone to find out who to address it to). In your letter you should show that you know something about the company. A good example is shown on the right.

BEWARE!

You will need to stress all your good points on your CV, but you must be honest. If you get an interview, you will be asked lots of questions about what is on your CV, so if you exaggerated anything, you will soon be found out.

your address

the employer's address

Always write to a named person.

today's date

Explain what you are applying for.

Explain why you are applying.

Say that you have enclosed your CV and don't forget to enclose it.

Always use "sincerely" when writing to a named person.

Don't forget to sign your letter!

Manhar Sanghi
39 Spalding Road
Birmingham B22 9FG
Tel 0121 610 4912

23 January 2007

Mr Anthony Spear
The Travel Company
Coventry Hospital
24 Shepton Road
Coventry CV41 6FS

Dear Mr Spear

With reference to your advertisment in the Birmingham Post on 15 January 2007 I am writing to apply for the post of Children's Holiday Representative.

I have always wanted to work with children, and my experience working as a pool attendant will be beneficial for working as a children's holiday representative in one of your resorts.

As requested I have enclosed my CV. I am available for interview at any time and can start work as soon as required. I look forward to hearing from you.

Yours sincerely

Manhar Sanghi

Interviews

Employers interview many people to try and find the best person for the job. You therefore have to show the interviewer that *you* are that person.

There are a number of things you can do to prepare yourself for an interview. First, find out everything you can about the company and what the job involves. You can then prepare some questions to ask the interviewer about the job – after all, the interview is also an opportunity for you to find out about that particular job and company.

Get ahead!

Write down some other examples of your skills that fall into the following categories:
- dealing with people
- team work
- practical skills
- organizing.

Now try to imagine how you would use these skills in the organization you have applied to. The interviewer will want to see how you will fit into the team.

You should read through your application form or CV to remind yourself of how you answered any questions. The interviewer is bound to ask you questions related to the information you have given, so be prepared.

left: *In an interview, be as prepared, as relaxed, and as confident as you can.*

On the day of the interview, dress smartly and make sure your appearance is neat and tidy, otherwise an employer will not be impressed. Arrive for the interview 10 minutes early, so you will not be worried about being late.

In the interview itself the most important thing to do is relax and be yourself. Be enthusiastic and answer all the questions clearly. If you do not understand a question ask the interviewer to explain it, and don't worry if you do not know the answer to a question. Just be honest and do not make things up. Remember to be positive and sell yourself.

SOME COMMON INTERVIEW QUESTIONS

Think of answers to these questions before you go for an interview. They are the type of questions interviewers like to ask.

◎ Why do you want this job?
◎ Why do you think you would be good at this job?
◎ What are your strengths and weaknesses?
◎ What did you like about your work experience?
◎ What did you learn from your work experience?
◎ What do you think are the important qualities for this job?
◎ What do you know about this company?
◎ How would your friends or family describe you?
◎ Do you work well in a team and can you give any examples?
◎ How do you stay organized?
◎ What do you think would be the worst part of this job?

When the interview is over, it is unlikely that you will find out if you got the job straight away. The company will usually have lots more people to interview before a decision is made. When you do get the result, do not give up if you are unsuccessful – after all, you may have come a close second. Ask the interviewer for feedback. This way you should be able to work out why you didn't get the job and will be able to do better next time.

Chapter 7

Onwards and upwards

Imagine that you have done well at school, obtained all the relevant qualifications, skills, and experience, applied for your ideal job in the leisure and tourism industry, and been successful. Congratulations! So what happens now? How do you shape you career? What opportunities are there for further training and advancement?

Ongoing training while at work

Most employers will provide some form of on-the-job training when you start working for them. Once you are settled in your job there may be further opportunities to train at work and you should take advantage of these. In order to do well in your chosen career, and hopefully to move onwards and upwards, it is a good idea to get as much training as possible. Some of the types of training offered by employers are described opposite.

above: *Ongoing training while at work is essential for making sure you are up to date with new developments, for example, in first-aid techniques.*

Fitness instructor

Once you become a qualified fitness instructor your name can go on the National Fitness Register. You will need to keep up to date with advances in exercise techniques and the correct use of equipment. As a swimming teacher you also need to keep up to date with new teaching methods. You can become a member of the Institute of Swim Teachers to keep informed.

CASE STUDY

James is a freelance aerobics teacher.

I have to organize my own training as I work for myself. This is very easy to do, though, as there are lots of training modules available for instructors. I have taken modules in Kick Aerobics, Step Aerobics, Body Conditioning and Seniors Aerobics (which teaches safe steps for older people). These modules can last anything from a day up to 4 weeks. I am looking into doing Sports Therapy and Pilates as my next modules. There are also workshops around the country with international presenters and fitness weekends to go to.

Where do I go next?

Your prospects for promotion depend on your ability and performance in your job. Many jobs offer the opportunity for promotion to supervisory or managerial levels. There are plenty of opportunities to work abroad and in some jobs it is possible to become self-employed.

left: *Being a manager is possible in many leisure and tourism careers.*

Holiday companies

As a rep or tour guide, promotion opportunities are few. Most people work in this field for only a few seasons and then move on to a new job that offers employment for the whole year. However, companies will want to hold on to good members of staff. In some large companies it is possible to gain promotion to senior posts, for example, senior resort representative or regional manager. If you are a tour guide employed by a company you could progress from tour guide to tour manager.

CASE STUDY

Rili is a head holiday representative in a Greek resort.

The company provides a short induction training programme for resort representatives in the UK. Once in the resort, experienced staff often provide training and support for an initial period.

When I started working abroad I received training in Spanish and Greek. I have become more fluent while working in these places. Having a good grasp of the local language is invaluable, as not only do you gain a great deal of respect from the locals, but it also allows you to communicate efficiently and effectively. This results in a far smoother operation and also maintains good working relations.

Since moving to my present position as team leader, I've attended a week's intensive management training course, including health and safety issues.

Tourist information and travel agents

If you work in a tourist information centre or travel agency, you could move into management at branch level. From there, you could move into the different levels of management within the tourist board or head office of a large travel agency. It may be necessary to move from branch to branch or from employer to employer in order to progress. You could also move **sideways** into other jobs within the tourism industry, such as a resort representative or tour guide. Some travel consultants move on to open their own online independent travel company, often working from home.

Sarah is the manager of a small independent travel agency.

I started my career in a large high street travel agency as a trainee travel consultant with the Modern Apprenticeship scheme. Within a year of finishing my training I had been promoted to senior sales consultant level, and then 2 years later became an assistant manager. Then I applied for the post of manager at a different travel agency and got the job. Being in charge of my own shop is like a dream come true for me.

Cinemas

Possibilities for promotion within a cinema are also limited. After gaining experience you may get promoted into a supervisory job, but there are few posts at managerial level.

Leisure centres

After gaining experience, health and fitness instructors and pool attendants can progress to supervisory or managerial posts, such as senior recreation assistant, duty manager, or general pool manager. With further training it may be possible to move into the field of training new fitness instructors or pool attendants, or to become a swimming teacher or sports coach.

If you are already in a management position in a leisure centre, after obtaining further experience you might gain promotion to deputy manager and then to manager. You could also move from managing a smaller centre to managing a larger one, or even to managing a group of centres.

TRANSFERABLE SKILLS

People who succeed in the leisure and tourism industry develop a range of communication and people skills that can also be useful in other jobs. Within the industry there are plenty of opportunities at all levels for you to create an interesting career for yourself. However, for some there may come a time when you feel the need to move out of the industry, and these so-called **transferable skills** will enable you to do that.

Conclusion

So, are you still interested in pursuing a career in leisure and tourism? The industry can certainly offer you a challenging and varied career with plenty of opportunities for promotion. You will have to work hard to get there though, as a lot of people see leisure and tourism as an attractive industry to work in.

Many people also think that working in this area will be like one endless holiday. You know better than that! You know that for many jobs in leisure and tourism the work is not always as exciting or as glamorous as it sounds. You know that the hours you work are likely to be long, and that you will have to work for very modest amounts of money at the beginning of your career. You also know that you will have to work some evenings and weekends, when you would much rather be out having a good time with your friends.

right: Picking a career you enjoy is one of the most important decisions you will make in your life – make sure you think carefully about it!

above: *Theme parks offer a huge variety of jobs.*

Making the right choice

You need to think very carefully about what you want from your career. Different people want different things, and the sooner you decide what you want to do, the sooner you can start working towards gaining the relevant qualifications.

You also need to decide if you are the right person to enjoy working in this industry. It is certainly not for everyone. For most jobs, your personality will be more important than the qualifications you have gained. It is possible to find employment in some leisure and tourism jobs without any qualifications at all. However, as competition for jobs is likely to be strong, it is an advantage for you to have qualifications as well as the right personality. As if this is not enough already, you also need to have some work experience, particularly of working with the public. Once you have all this under your belt you will be well placed for applying for a job in the leisure and tourism industry. Then all you need to do is stand out from the crowd!

This industry is very diverse, with a huge range of jobs on offer. The range of jobs is also increasing, as people have more leisure time and more money to spend on their leisure. In fact, the leisure and tourism industry is the world's fastest-growing, job-creating profession. It is not surprising that you think you would like to be a part of it all!

Jobs in leisure and tourism

- ◎ Aerobics instructor
- ◎ Airline attendant
- ◎ Art gallery manager
- ◎ Campsite receptionist
- ◎ Cinema attendant
- ◎ Cruise ship entertainer
- ◎ Ground staff
- ◎ Health and fitness instructor
- ◎ Health club manager
- ◎ Holiday home letter
- ◎ Leisure centre manager
- ◎ Life guard
- ◎ Museum guide
- ◎ Park warden
- ◎ PE teacher
- ◎ Pool attendant
- ◎ Recreation assistant
- ◎ Resort representative
- ◎ Ride operator
- ◎ Sports coach
- ◎ Swimming teacher
- ◎ Theatre usher
- ◎ Tour guide
- ◎ Tourist information centre assistant
- ◎ Travel consultant

Please note that qualifications and courses are subject to change.

Careers websites

◎ City and Guilds (www.city-and-guilds.co.uk)
  – This website tells you all about City and Guilds qualifications.

◎ Connexions Direct (www.connexions-direct.com)
  – This website gives advice to young people, including learning and careers. Includes link to the Jobs4U careers database.

◎ Learndirect (www.learndirect-advice.co.uk) and Learndirect Scotland (www.learndirectscotland.com/)
  – Go to "job profiles" for details of many jobs in leisure and tourism and courses and qualifications.

◎ Modern Apprenticeships, Scotland
  (www.scottish-enterprise.com/modernapprenticeships)
  – Check out the case studies of people already training.

◎ Need2Know: Learning (www.need2know.co.uk/learning)
  – This site gives information about studying and qualifications.

◎ Qualifications and Curriculum Authority (www.qca.org.uk/14-19)
  – Go to "Qualifications" and click on "Main qualification groups" to find out about NVQs.

◎ Scottish Vocational Qualifications (www.sqa.org.uk)
  – You can find out all the latest qualifications information here.

◎ The National Council for Work Experience
  (www.work-experience.org)
  – Go to "Students and Graduates" to search for placements.

Get ahead in leisure and tourism!

◎ Association of British Travel Agents (www.abta.com)
◎ Association of Professional Tourist Guides (www.aptg.org.uk)
◎ British Association of Leisure Parks, Piers, and Attractions (www.balppa.org)
◎ British Tourist Authority (www.visitbritain.com)
◎ English Tourism Council (www.englishtourism.org.uk)
◎ Guild of Business Travel Agents (www.gbta-guild.com)
◎ Institute of Travel and Tourism (www.itt.co.uk)
◎ People 1st (www.people1st.co.uk)
◎ Springboard UK (www.springboarduk.org.uk)
◎ Travel Training Company (www.ttctraining.co.uk)

administration managing and organizing a company

anatomy study of the human body

apprenticeship training scheme that allows you to work for money, learn, and become qualified at the same time

Blue Badge qualification British national standard tour guide qualification

budget plan of how a company will spend its money

casual work work that only lasts for a short period of time

chalet mountain house, usually near ski slopes

cinema auditorium room in a cinema where films are shown

coach someone who trains people in a sport

commentary description of something

commission amount of money paid to someone for a service

conservation preservation or restoration of the environment and/or wildlife

crèche place where babies are looked after

culture customs of a society or country

currency type of money that a country uses

facility building, room, or piece of equipment used for an activity

foreign exchange place where you can buy and sell foreign money

freelance self-employed rather than working for a company

growth industry industry that is developing rapidly

Higher National Certificate (HNC) technical qualification that you can take after a National Certificate or after A-levels/Highers

Higher National Diploma (HND) technical qualification that you progress to from an HNC (see HNC). Usually takes 2 years to achieve.

holiday/resort representative person who works in a holiday resort on behalf of a travel company. "Reps" are there to help and entertain holidaymakers.

humid hot, wet air

initiative ability to make your own decisions

isolated feeling alone

kibbutz farm in Israel where many people live and work together

leisure time when you are not working or at school

Masters second or further degree

Modern Apprenticeship Scottish apprenticeship, lasts for 4 years

motivate make someone want to do something

national park area of countryside protected by the state for the enjoyment of the general public or preservation of the environment and/or wildlife

National Trust organization concerned to preserve historic monuments and buildings and places of historical interest or natural beauty

National Vocational Qualification (NVQ) in England and Wales, a work-related, competence-based qualification that shows you have the knowledge and skills to do a job effectively. NVQs represent national standards that are recognized by employers throughout the UK.

nutrition getting the right kind of food for good health

on call prepared to work if you are needed

passport official document used by the government to identify the holder's citizenship and entitle them to travel abroad under its protection

perk extra advantage that you may be given when you work for a company, for example, free private healthcare

permit official document giving permission to do something

promotion move to a more important job in an organization

retired stopped working, usually because of old age

salary money that you receive as payment from the organization you work for

Scottish Vocational Qualification (SVQ) in Scotland, a work-related, competence-based qualification that shows you have the knowledge and skills to do a job effectively. SVQs represent national standards that are recognized by employers throughout the UK.

seasonal lasts for a season, for example, the summer or winter season

service help that is given to someone

sideways move to a new job or position, but remain at the same level

stately home large, historical house

sublet when the tenant of a rented property rents part or all of the property to another tenant

tolerant allow people to do what they want without criticizing them

tourism business of providing services to people while they are on hoilday

transferable skills skills that you have learnt at school or in a job that can be used in another job

travel insurance protection against something bad happening, such as an accident, while you are on holiday

vaccination often an injection, which protects against disease

volunteer person who offers to do a job or service without payment

Young Men's Christian Assocation (YMCA) organization set up to develop young people in mind, body, and spirit

Index